THE *Vega* New *Parents'* GUIDE

By Juliet Gellatley BSc, DIP CNM, founder & director, Viva!
Recipes by Helen Wilson

© Viva! 2022. Fourth Update
(previously *Vegetarian & Vegan Mother and Baby Guide*)
Recipe photography by Maryanne Hall
Registered charity 1037486

Produced by:
Viva!, 8 York Court, Wilder St, Bristol BS2 8QH
Tel: 0117 944 1000
E: info@viva.org.uk

viva.org.uk
viva.org.uk/health
veganrecipeclub.org.uk
f vivavegancharity
y vivacampaigns
◎ vivacharity

Juliet has a a degree in zoology and is a qualified nutritional therapist. She founded and directs Viva! and is an authority on vegan health and nutrition, as well as other vegan issues.

She is the mum of twin sons (Jazz and Finn) and so understands vegan pregnancy and weaning first hand! Juliet has led many campaigns on vegan issues and given hundreds of public talks, media appearances and is author of several books, reports and guides.

Helen Wilson (Viva!'s Recipes for Toddlers section) is a vegan chef and writer who has spent the last 13 years promoting, teaching and creating vegan food. While working for Viva! she delivered dozens of talks and cookery demonstrations across the UK and her recipes have appeared in many major food magazines, books and websites. Helen is mum to two boys, vegan since birth, and so has a wealth of knowledge on vegan pregnancy, weaning and beyond. She runs a plant-based coffee bar in South Wales.

Viva!
H E A L T H

4

Contents

Pregnancy

A balanced vegan diet provides all the nutrients needed for a healthy pregnancy. Healthy babies are being born to eighth and ninth generation vegetarians and vegans in the UK and of course, around the world, whole cultures have been vegetarian for thousands of years! It is the most natural, healthful diet and perfect for nurturing your unborn child. If you would like more easy-to-read and reassuring information on what is a natural, healthy diet for mums-to-be and all people, read Viva!'s guide, *Vegan for Health*.

A healthy pregnancy should just be an extension of your normally healthy diet. If you eat well anyway, then eating right for your unborn child won't be such a radical change. If, however, your diet has always been based around junk food, meat and dairy produce, then it's time it wasn't! For both your sakes.

The secret of a healthy diet is to eat a variety of foods focusing on wholegrains, pulses (peas, beans and lentils of all types), unsalted mixed nuts and seeds, fresh fruit and vegetables. The table on page 8 shows what you need to eat each day. Eggs, meat, milk and cheese are high in cholesterol, animal fats and hormones (cow's milk contains 35 hormones and growth factors!) and are not needed (or even desirable) for a healthy diet, so they are not included.

There is plenty of scope for adventurous, creative cookery. With herbs, spices, stock cubes, flavourings such as soya sauce and creamed coconut, plant-based cheese and a host of other extras, you can create the most wonderfully exotic dishes, as well as all the traditional favourites.

WHAT TO EACH DAY FOR HEALTH —
PRE AND POST PREGNANCY

(Nutrients are increased during pregnancy – see below.)

1

NO. OF SERVINGS **At least 5**

FOODS Fruit and vegetables

TO PROVIDE Healthy energy, vitamin A, vitamin C, vitamin K, folate, calcium, iron, fibre and many antioxidants!

HEALTHY PORTION SIZE

Fresh Fruit	1 medium piece – the size of a tennis ball
Dried Fruit	1-1½ tablespoons or the size of a golf ball
Green or Root Veg	3 tablespoons
Salad Veg	80 grams or a large cereal bowl

2

NO. OF SERVINGS **3-5**

FOODS Wholegrains and cereals

TO PROVIDE Energy, fibre, B vitamins, calcium, iron, protein

HEALTHY PORTION SIZE

Cooked brown rice, couscous or other grains	2-3 heaped tablespoons or ½ cup
Breakfast cereal	1 regular sized cereal bowl
Wholewheat pasta	1 cup (cooked) as side dish or 2 cups as main dish
Wholemeal bread	2 slices

3

NO. OF SERVINGS **3-4**

FOODS Pulses, nuts or seeds

TO PROVIDE Protein, energy, healthy fats, fibre, calcium, iron, other minerals and antioxidants

HEALTHY PORTION SIZE

Peas, beans, chickpeas	½ cup (cooked) and lentils
Tofu, mock meats, burgers, sausages	100 grams or one serving (burger or sausage)
Nuts or seeds	2 tablespoons or a small handful

NO. OF SERVINGS **Small Amounts**

FOODS Healthy oils

TO PROVIDE Energy, vitamin E (vegetable oils), vitamins A & D (fortified margarine), essential omega-3 and omega-6 fats (flaxseed, walnut, hemp)

HEALTHY PORTION SIZE

Flaxseed, hempseed, walnut oil	1 tbsp used cold
Rapeseed oil	1 tbsp for cooking
Virgin olive oil	1 tbsp used cold
Plant-based margarine	Small amounts

4

NO. OF SERVINGS **Daily dose**

FOODS Vitamin B12, Vitamin D

TO PROVIDE Vitamin B12

HEALTHY PORTION SIZE These are vital to give as supplements – 50 micrograms of vitamin B12 and 10 micrograms of vitamin D

FOODS Omega-3 fats

HEALTHY PORTION SIZE 1 tsp flaxseed oil / 1tbsp ground flaxseed or chia seeds / 2 tbsp of hempseed / 10 walnut halves. Children aged 1-3 should get a daily omega-3 supplement made from algae

5

Aim for one to two litres of water each day. Add a slice of lemon, other fruit or fresh mint. Squash can contribute but unsweetened drinks (eg fruit or herbal tea) are better

* **Note on Nuts**: Pregnant or lactating women from atopic families – where classical allergies such as asthma, hay-fever, urticaria (skin rashes), rhinitis (recurrent sneezing and watering of the nose) or eczema exist in family members – should avoid peanuts (actually a pulse) and nuts in their own diet as sensitisation to these foods can occur in the womb and through breastfeeding. These foods should not be introduced into the diet of infants of such atopic mothers until at least three years of age or at a time recommended by a doctor. However for the majority of infants peanuts and nuts are an important addition to the diet and can be introduced into the diet from six months of age provided they are of a suitable texture such as smooth nut butters. Whole nuts should not be given to children under five years of age due to the risk of choking.

BEiNG UNDER OR OVERWEiGHT AFFECTS YOUR BABY

Many studies show that mums who under eat increase their child's risk of developing obesity and related diseases (eg heart disease, diabetes and cancer). It is believed that the foetus makes physiological adaptations to the 'famine' to prepare him or herself for life after birth. Far from being protective, these changes make the child more vulnerable to obesity and disease.

Recent research has also shown that mums who eat a high fat and/or high sugar diet during pregnancy risks their baby being predisposed to obesity and their children having metabolic syndrome (the precursor to type 2 diabetes).

To state the obvious, it's important to not under or overeat during pregnancy! And it's important to eat the right types of foods.

DO YOU NEED TO EAT TWICE AS MUCH WHEN PREGNANT?

In short, no!

But during pregnancy a woman has to provide good nutrition for two individuals. The growing baby gets all his/her nourishment from mum through the umbilical cord, so diet is very important. If mum is lacking in any vitamins and nutrients, her baby might lack them too.

If a woman has had trouble keeping her weight up or down before the pregnancy, she should make a nutritional plan with the help of a nutritional therapist or midwife.

HOW MUCH ENERGY DOES A WOMAN NEED DURING PREGNANCY?

(Calories are sometimes called kilocalories or kcals.)

- A woman who is not pregnant needs approximately 2,100 calories per day.
- A pregnant woman needs approximately 2,500 calories per day.
- A breastfeeding woman needs approximately 3,000 calories per day.

INCREASING YOUR NUTRIENTS FOR PREGNANCY

During pregnancy, your daily nutrient requirements increase. Iron, folic acid, thiamine, niacin, riboflavin as well as vitamins A, C and D, calcium and protein, are all needed in greater amounts. It's not surprising – you're making a whole new person and you'll need more nutrients than you do normally (see above). If your diet includes plenty of fresh fruit and vegetables, you will probably be getting more than enough of vitamins A and C, folate and thiamine, but it doesn't hurt to give them all a bit of a boost.

The recommended amount of fruit and veg we should all eat is of course five a day – but this is the minimum, not the maximum! Aim for five to eight portions daily. If you find that challenging – buy a juicer. They range in price from about £50 to several hundred but are a great investment because fruit and vegetable juices are a wonderful source of many vitamins, minerals and trace elements, including iron, calcium, zinc and folic acid. Experiment with different combinations for a vitamin-packed, energy boosting drink!

Make it part of your routine to juice any fruit you enjoy – try apples, pears, tangerines with any berries (fresh or frozen) for a huge vitamin and antioxidant boost! About five of these fruits makes a small-medium glass of juice and tastes phenomenally good. Also try mixing fruit and veg together such as carrots with apples and a little ginger root for zest and even more goodness. Visit Viva!'s Vegan Recipe Club online or via the app for lots more ideas.

Here's more on how to boost your intake of important nutrients during pregnancy...

FABULOUS FOODS FOR FEMALE FERTILITY & PREGNANCY

VITAMINS

NUTRIENT **Beta Carotene** (forms Vitamin A)

WHY THEY'RE VITAL FOR A HEALTHY BABY & PREGNANCY

Crucial for enzymes for implantation of your fertilised egg. Essential for growth and development of foetus including his or her heart, lungs, kidneys, bones and for hearing and vision. Also needed for infection resistance, fat metabolism and red blood cell production.

Helps keep DNA (genetic blueprint) healthy. Vitamin A is crucial for women about to give birth, as it helps with postpartum tissue repair.

RICH SOURCES Mangoes, Apricots, Peaches, Cantaloupe Melons, Watermelon, Carrots, Sweet Potatoes, Red/Yellow Peppers, Tomatoes, Green Leafy Vegetables (eg Broccoli, Cabbage, Spinach, Brussels Sprouts, Bok choy), Watercress, Pumpkins, Romaine Lettuce, Chestnuts and Pistachio nuts.

NUTRIENT **B Vitamins**

WHY THEY'RE VITAL FOR A HEALTHY BABY & PREGNANCY

Vital for making your sex hormones. Needed for converting food into energy. For creating new blood cells for growing baby and aiding growth, healthy vision and skin. Essential for your baby's nerve, brain, bone and muscle development.

Vitamin B6 can help reduce morning sickness (Beans, Nuts, Avocados and Bananas are good sources).

RICH SOURCES Wholegrains (Wheat, Rice, Oats, Rye, Buckwheat, Barley etc); Beansprouts, Pulses (Lentils, Beans and Peas of all types inc Soya Beans and French Beans), Avocados, Bananas, Potatoes, Sweet Potatoes, Mushrooms, Red Peppers, Carrots, Cabbage, Nuts (eg Peanuts, Almonds, Brazil Nuts) and Quinoa. Different B vitamins are in different foods so variety is the key.

Vitamin B9 (folic acid)

Vital for prevention of spina bifida and other neural tube defects and needed in first 28 days of pregnancy – so you need to take from preconception. If you are pregnant or thinking of having a baby, consider taking a daily 0.4 milligram (400 microgram) folic acid supplement from the time you stop using contraception until the twelfth week of pregnancy. Also supports the placenta.

RICH SOURCES Berries, Mangoes, Pineapples, Avocados, Green Leafy Vegetables, Cauliflower, Asparagus, Parsnips, Pulses (eg Peas, Chickpeas, Kidney Beans, Black Eyed Beans, Edamame & Soya products such as Tofu, Lentils), Brown Rice, Seeds (eg Sunflower Seeds), and Fortified Breakfast Cereals.

NUTRIENT **Vitamin C**

WHY THEY'RE VITAL FOR A HEALTHY BABY & PREGNANCY

Essential for formation of collagen (in pregnancy keeps protective membrane around baby strong). Collagen is also a component of skin, cartilage, tendons and bones. Also helps fight infections and cell damage. Helps you absorb iron. Mum and baby need a daily supply of this vitamin.

RICH SOURCES Blackcurrants, Kiwis, Mangoes, Oranges, Papayas, Grapefruits, Passion Fruits, Pineapples, Strawberries, Lychees, Chestnuts, Avocados, Butternut Squash, Broccoli, Spinach, Cabbage, Swiss Chard, Brussels Sprouts, Bell Peppers (any colour), Parsley, Potatoes, Peas and many other fresh fruit & green vegetables.

Vitamin D

Essential for tooth enamel and bone development in your developing baby. A deficiency during pregnancy can slow growth and cause skeletal deformities, putting baby at risk of developing rickets after birth.

In spring and summer, most people in the UK get enough vitamin D through the action of sunlight on the skin, but during the winter months a supplement is required.

Vitamin E

Protects vital genetic blueprint (RNA and DNA) reducing risk of congenital defects.

Apples, Berries (all types), Kiwis, Mangoes, Nectarines, Peaches, Vegetable Oils, Wheatgerm, Wholegrains, Tomatoes, Nuts (especially Almonds and Hazelnuts), Sunflower Seeds, Pine Nuts, Avocados, Asparagus, Butternut Squash, Parsnips, Potatoes, Spinach, Carrots and Celery.

Vitamin K

Supplied by food but main source is from gut bacteria. Baby is born sterile so must rely on mum's supply from breast milk or formula milk for several weeks. Eat plenty of dark green veg.

Avocados, Berries, Pears, Kiwis, Mangoes, Pomegranates, Broccoli, Lettuces, Cucumbers, Celery, Carrots, Asparagus, Spinach, Cabbage, Brussels Sprouts, Bok Choy, Leeks, Edamame, Kidney Beans, Molasses, Peas, Basil, Thyme, Nuts (eg Cashews, Chestnuts, Hazelnuts and Pistachios).

MINERALS & TRACE ELEMENTS

NUTRIENT Calcium

WHY THEY'RE VITAL FOR A HEALTHY BABY & PREGNANCY

For development of baby's bones, heart, muscles and nervous system, also heart rhythm and blood clotting. If you don't get enough calcium when you're pregnant, your baby will draw it from your bones, which may weaken your health later on. Therefore it is also important to reduce the risk of oesteoporosis in mum later on in life.

RICH SOURCES Non-oxalate dark green leafy vegetables (eg Broccoli, Kale, Spring Greens, Cabbage, Bok Choy, Parsley and Watercress), Dried Fruits (eg Figs and Dates), Nuts (particularly Almonds and Brazil Nuts), Coconuts, Seeds including Sesame Seeds and Tahini (sesame seed paste) used to make Hummus, Quinoa, Pulses (any Peas, Beans and Lentils) and calcium-set Tofu (Soya Bean Curd), Root Veg (eg Parsnips, Swedes, Turnips), Olives, Calcium-enriched Plant-based Milk (check the ingredients label for calcium – most soya milks contain the same amount of calcium as cow's milk).

NUTRIENT Chromium

WHY THEY'RE VITAL FOR A HEALTHY BABY & PREGNANCY

Essential in controlling blood sugar levels and helps make DNA (genetic building blocks in every cell). Promotes the building of proteins in your developing baby's growing tissues.

RICH SOURCES Onions, Tomatoes, Romaine Lettuce, Potatoes, Lentils, Wholegrains (Wholegrain Bread, Oats, Rye, Barley, Brown Rice), Spices (eg Black Pepper and Thyme).

Iron

One-third of pregnant women in Britain develop mild anaemia. Iron is needed to make haemoglobin, the protein in red blood cells that carries oxygen to every cell in your body for energy and growth. The amount of blood in your body increases during pregnancy until you have almost 50 per cent more than usual (even more if twins!), so you need more iron to make more haemoglobin. Mum supplies oxygen to baby via her placenta. Iron also helps build bones and teeth. If mum doesn't have enough iron then baby may be in short supply.

RICH SOURCES Dried Apricots, Prunes, Raisins, Figs, Dates, Cherries, Grapes, Blackcurrants, Blackberries, Raspberries, Strawberries, Lychees, Watermelon, Avocados, Broccoli, Bok Choy, Spinach, Cabbage, Pumpkins, Pulses (all types of Beans, Peas and Lentils), French Beans, Wholegrains (esp. Oats, Rye, Wholewheat and Spelt), Pumpkin Seeds, Quinoa, Coconut Flesh, Black Treacle, Cocoa, Turmeric and Thyme.

NUTRIENT Magnesium

WHY THEY'RE VITAL FOR A HEALTHY BABY & PREGNANCY

For energy production, healthy bones and liver, to help balance blood sugars, relax muscles, for nerve function, and for many hormones including stress hormones. Healthy levels of magnesium during pregnancy can help keep the womb from contracting prematurely.

RICH SOURCES Apricots, Apples, Bananas, Prunes, Berries (eg Blackberries, Raspberries), Watermelons, Green Leafy Veg (eg Broccoli, Bok Choy, Spinach, Cabbage, Brussels Sprouts), Nuts (eg Almonds, Brazil Nuts, Cashews), Pulses (esp. all types of beans), Avocados, Artichokes, French Beans, Butternut Squash, Wholegrains and Quinoa.

Phosphorus

Needed for building baby's bones and teeth; normal heart rhythm and developing blood clotting. Also for healthy kidneys, nervous system, repairing cells and creating and using energy.

RICH SOURCES Avocados, Blackcurrants, Passion Fruits, Pomegranates, Dried Fruit (eg Dates), Artichokes, Potatoes, Celeriac, French Beans, Parsnips, Nuts, Pulses (all types of Peas, Beans and Lentils), Wholegrains, Garlic and Quinoa.

Potassium

Important for muscle activity and contractions, heart muscle and nerve function and making energy. During pregnancy it protects against high blood pressure and osteoporosis as it lowers the loss of calcium from the bones.

RICH SOURCES Bananas, Cantaloupe Melons, Apricots, Strawberries, Fennel, Brussels Sprouts, Broccoli, Aubergines, Tomatoes, Parsley, Cucumbers, Turmeric, Ginger Root, Avocados, Cauliflower, Cabbage, Nuts (eg Almonds) and Coconuts.

Selenium

Protective against free radical damage to cells and risk of congenital defects. Helps fight heavy metal poisoning.

RICH SOURCES Brazil Nuts (very high), Bananas, Mangoes, Watermelon, Asparagus, French Beans, Parsnips, Wholegrains, Garlic, Brewer's Yeast, Sweetcorn, Spinach, Broccoli, Pulses (Peas, Beans and Lentils), Brewer's Yeast and Mushrooms.

Zinc

Probably plays biggest role in reproduction. Deficiency increases miscarriage rate, low birth weight, labour and delivery problems. Needed for hormone balance, development of egg, successful fertilisation and enzymes of egg implantation. Zinc is important for enzymes to work and helps make insulin. It is needed to create and repair DNA (genetic blueprint) so getting enough zinc is important for the rapid cell growth that occurs during pregnancy. Also helps form nerves, skeleton, organs and circulatory system. Needed for a healthy immune system and sense of taste and smell.

RICH SOURCES Avocados, Blackberries, Raspberries, Asparagus, French Beans, Brussels Sprouts, Pulses (Peas, Beans and Lentils of all types inc cocoa beans in dark chocolate and cocoa powder), Wholegrains (eg Brown Rice, Wholemeal Bread, Oats, Rye), Green Leafy Veg, Nuts (eg Peanuts), Seeds (especially Pumpkin Seeds, Sesame Seeds used to make Hummus), Brewer's Yeast, Basil and Thyme.

NUTRIENT **Carbohydrates**

Your (and so your baby's) main source of energy! Eats lots of complex carbs.

RICH SOURCES Wholegrains (Oats, Wholemeal Bread, Brown Rice, Pasta eg Wholemeal Spaghetti), Rye, Potatoes, Sweet Potatoes, Pulses (all Beans, Peas & Lentils).

Fats

Good fats are vital for your baby's brain and eye development before and after birth. They also help the placenta and other tissues grow and may help stop premature birth and low birth weight.

RICH SOURCES Seeds especially Ground Flaxseed (aka Linseed), Hempseed and their Oils, Nuts & Nut Oils (especially Walnuts), Virgin Olive Oil, Dark Green Leafy Vegetables, Soya Beans (eg Tofu), Avocados. Sunflower and olive oil are good for cooking. Flaxseed and hempseed oil shouldn't be heated. Ideal for salad dressing though and high in omega-3!

NUTRIENT **Fibre**

WHY THEY'RE VITAL FOR A HEALTHY BABY & PREGNANCY

During pregnancy, the body produces more female hormones than normal and this can cause constipation. Fibre is vital for healthy bowels and bowel movement.

RICH SOURCES All Fresh Fruit & Vegetables, Dried Fruits (eg Prunes and Apricots) Wholegrains (eg Pasta, Rice, Oats, Bread, Barley and Rye), All Nuts, All Pulses (eg Beans, Peas and Lentils – baked beans are high).

NUTRIENT **Protein**

WHY THEY'RE VITAL FOR A HEALTHY BABY & PREGNANCY

Protein is vital to build and repair your and your baby's cells. It's particularly important to get enough protein throughout your second and third trimesters, when your baby is growing the fastest and your breasts and organs are getting bigger to fulfil the needs of your growing baby.

RICH SOURCES Pulses (eg Peas, Beans and Lentils), Soya (eg Tofu, Soya Milk and Soya Mince), Wholegrains (eg Brown Rice, Wholemeal Bread and Pasta, Oats and Rye), Seeds (all types) & Seed Paste (eg Tahini used in Hummus), Beansprouts and Nuts (all types).

"When I found out I was pregnant, I knew that I would be having a vegan pregnancy. Naturally, I had lots of questions – is veganism healthy during pregnancy? Which supplements should I be taking? Are there any foods I should avoid? Viva!'s Vegan New Parents' guide gave me all the reassurance I needed and more! It clearly explained why veganism is the healthiest choice for my baby and provided delicious recipes for all stages of pregnancy and beyond.

Packed with useful charts and statistics, I feel better-informed and supported throughout my pregnancy – with no doubt that I am making the right choice for me and my baby. I look forward to using the guide throughout all the ups and down of motherhood – from breastfeeding, to non-dairy formula, to weaning and food preparation, I know that Viva! has all the information available in an easy-to-understand way. I've had a very easy, textbook pregnancy, with thanks to my vegan diet and the Viva! New Parents' guide."
Roisin McAuley

PROTEIN

Protein is needed for growth, repair of tissue and protection against infection. Protein can be found in all pulses (all types of beans, peas and lentils), nuts, seeds, brown rice, wholegrains and wholegrain products such as breakfast cereals, wholemeal bread and wholewheat pasta. The humble soya bean – used in many soya products such as soya burgers, soya milk and tofu (soya bean curd) is nutritionally equivalent to meat, containing as it does all the building blocks (amino acids) of protein. Try cooking the unadulterated green young soya beans (called edamame in Japanese restaurants and in freezers of many supermarkets) as a starter or side dish – delicious!

The seed quinoa is also high in protein, containing all essential amino acids and so, as with soya, is known as a complete protein. Use it like a grain – many people use it in place of rice or potatoes in stir-fries, soups and so on. It's easy to cook, taking about 15 minutes to prepare. It's available in most supermarkets.

Preeclampsia, a syndrome of high blood pressure, reduced blood flow to the placenta and premature delivery, has been attributed to insufficient protein intake and so it is prudent to increase your intake in the final trimester. The good news – medical studies on 775 vegan mothers showed them to be less prone to preeclampsia.

FATS

Fats can either be saturated (found in high concentrations in most animal-derived foods such as butter, hard cheeses, red and white meats etc) or unsaturated. Whilst it's best not to eat the saturated kind at all we do need the unsaturated type – the so-called essential fatty acids or polyunsaturated fats. There are two types of essential fatty acids – omega-3 and omega-6.

These fats are essential in the diet for brain function, repairing body tissue, to carry some vitamins (vitamins A, D, E and K) and for manufacturing some hormones. Essential fatty acids are a main constituent of the brain and eyes and are vital for the healthy functioning of all cell membranes. Omega-3 is also particularly anti-inflammatory and important in combating many diseases such as heart disease and arthritis – plant omega-3s being the most powerful source (see Viva!'s guide, *Fish-Free for Life: Why Plant Omega-3s are Better for You and the Environment* for more information at **viva.org.uk/resources**).

The developing foetus requires omega-3 fatty acids for cell membranes and physiological functions, as well as for the brain and retina of the eye. The foetus requires a constant supply of this from mum and so is dependent on the maternal supply.

The best plant source of omega-3 fats is flaxseed, also known as linseed. Try ground flaxseed (they must be ground, otherwise the seeds will go straight through your system without the fats being absorbed). You can buy them from health food shops and supermarkets. Try sprinkling them on your breakfast cereal. The other source is flaxseed oil. Don't cook with this oil as heat destroys the omega-3s; instead use it to make salad dressings and pour cold into soups/casseroles/pasta dishes etc after you have cooked them. Add about 1 teaspoon full.

Omega-3 fats are also found in hemp seeds and hemp oil (use as above), cold-pressed rapeseed (canola) oil, dark green leafy vegetables such as broccoli, some nuts eg walnuts and walnut oil (use cold-pressed oils unheated in salad dressings), soya beans and soya oil and wheat germ.

Omega-6 fats are found in seeds and their oils (again use unheated) such as sunflower, sesame, corn, grapeseed, hemp and rapeseed, some nuts (eg pecans, pistachios and walnuts), rice bran and soya beans.

Most Western diets tend to be high in the omega-6 fats but not so high in the omega-3 fats. We are supposed to eat four times as much omega-6 as omega-3 oils – but many of us eat 15 to 30 times more omega-6 than 3. It's a good idea therefore to make sure you include a wide range of the omega-3 rich foods in your diet. There are even some specially formulated oils that supply both the omega-3 and omega-6 fats in the right proportions available from most health food shops. Hemp seed oil and rapeseed oil naturally contain about the right proportions. Soya beans are pretty good too. Flaxseeds are much higher in omega-3 than 6 so is useful if you need to top up omega-3 levels.

Probably the best oil to cook with is virgin olive oil. Although it does not contain omega-3 and is low in omega-6, it is high in another beneficial non-essential fatty acid (omega-9), has many health benefits and is relatively stable when heated.

A note on omega-3s from fish. Basically, don't eat them! All pregnant women are strongly advised by government to limit their oily fish intake and to not take cod liver oil (see Foods and Drinks to Avoid on page 29).

CALCIUM

This vital element is needed for the healthy functioning of the nervous system, blood clotting and bone and tooth formation in both mother and baby. Seeds (especially sesame), nuts* (especially almonds*), dark green leafy vegetables and pulses such as beans of all types, lentils, chickpeas and tofu (made from soya beans) are particularly rich in calcium. Contrary to popular belief, drinking cow's milk is no guarantee of strong bones. The Harvard Nurses' Health Study, took 77,761 women, aged 34 to 59 and followed them for 12 years. The research found that those who got more calcium from milk actually had slightly, but significantly, more fractures, than those who drank little or no milk. Another study of elderly men and women in Sydney, Australia also showed that higher dairy product consumption was associated with increased fracture risk. Those with the highest dairy product consumption had approximately double the risk of hip fracture than those with the lowest consumption. Viva! has some other great guides covering these topics, including *The Incredible Vegan Health Report* and *Why You Don't Need Dairy*, both available from **vivashop.org.uk**

*See page 9 *Note on Nuts*

IRON

The need for iron increases during pregnancy because both mother and baby are busy creating new blood. The best sources are dried fruits eg figs, apricots, dates and prunes, nuts* and seeds, especially sunflower, pumpkin and sesame seeds and black treacle. Lentils, kidney beans, baked beans and other pulses, tofu and soya milk, hummus, cocoa, fortified breakfast cereals, wholewheat and wheatgerm, green leafy vegetables and wholegrains (brown rice, oats etc) are also useful sources. Because vitamin C greatly increases the absorption of iron from the food in your body, it is essential to make sure you are eating plenty of fresh fruit and vegetables. The British Medical Association states that vegetarians are no more prone to iron-deficiency anaemia than meat-eaters. More info available in our factsheet Ironing out the Facts at **viva.org.uk/materials/ironing-out-the-facts-fact-sheet**

VITAMINS A, C AND E

Vegans get plenty of vitamin A from eating foods containing beta-carotene. We convert beta-carotene into vitamin A in our bodies. Beta-carotene is high in carrots, sweet potatoes, red and yellow peppers, tomatoes, green leafy vegetables, watercress, mangoes, apricots, pumpkins, cantaloupe melons and romaine lettuce.

You'll find high amounts of vitamin C in kiwi fruit, berries and currants, fresh oranges, grapefruit, broccoli, spinach, cabbage, peas, blackcurrants, strawberries, green peppers and other fruit and vegetables. It's not in meat. Beta-carotene, vitamins C and E (this latter vitamin is found in vegetable oils, wholegrains, tomatoes, nuts* especially almonds*, asparagus, spinach, apples, carrots, celery and avocado) are antioxidants and help protect you from several diseases including heart disease, stroke, type 2 diabetes and cancer.

"My partner and I became vegan in 2016, so raising our children vegan was an easy decision for us. The benefits of being a vegan family for us include raising a child who is naturally compassionate towards animals, has a lighter tread upon our struggling planet, and thrives on a healthy plant-based diet. Faye was given soya-based formula from birth, which gave her all the nutrients she needed.

   She took to weaning very well, relishing smashed avocado, chia puddings and sweet potato purées. Now at 14 months, she will happily eat various vegetables, pasta dishes, tofu stir-fries and chilli made with kidney beans – although she will never turn down a yummy dairy-free chocolate treat either! It is so easy to get all the nutrients you need at any life stage on a vegan diet, and the Viva! Vegan New Parents' guide is a fantastic place to get information."
Amelia Banner

"Having been vegetarian since the age of 10 and then turning vegan in my late twenties, it was the most natural decision ever to carry on and enjoy a vegan pregnancy and then raise my children vegan. I breast-fed both boys, who are now four and nine years of age. Both of them have always broken through their weight and height charts and with a combination of mashed vegan foods and baby led weaning, they now both enjoy a wide variety of foods. They are fabulous, adventurous eaters who are living proof that children can absolutely thrive on vegan diets. The original Viva! Mother & Baby Guide helped me every step of the way with raising both my boys."
Helen Wilson

THE B VITAMINS

These vital vitamins comprise B1 (thiamine), B2 (riboflavin), B3 (niacin), B5 (pantothenic acid), B6 (pyridoxine), B7 (biotin), B9 (folic acid) and B12 (cobalamin). Many B vitamins are involved in releasing energy from food and help to aid growth and repair of the body. They are widely available in wholegrains including wholemeal bread, brown rice and wholewheat pasta, yeast extracts (eg Marmite or low salt Meridian yeast extract with added vitamin B12), pulses (eg peas, beans and lentils), nuts, seeds, dark green leafy vegetables, avocados and bananas. Many breakfast cereals are also fortified with B vitamins.

Folic acid (B9) is required for protein synthesis, formation of blood, metabolism of DNA (our genetic blueprint) and helps prevent neural tube defects in the developing foetus. It is therefore necessary before conception and during early pregnancy to help prevent this condition. It is found widely in most vegetables, especially dark green leafy vegetables, nuts, pulses (peas, beans and lentils) and avocados.

Vitamin B12 (cobalamin) is required for the maintenance of a healthy nervous system and normal blood formation. The liver has stores of B12 lasting up to three years and the body is also very efficient at reabsorbing it. Many common foods are fortified with B12 such as fortified breakfast cereals (check the ingredients label), yeast extracts, vegetable margarines and plant milks. However, we recommend taking a B12 supplement to ensure you are getting enough.

Vitamins B6, B12 and folic acid (B9) are also necessary for helping to keep the arteries healthy.

ViTAMiN D

Just 15 minutes of exposure to sunlight on the face and arms is all that is required by the body to manufacture vitamin D. This vitamin aids the body's absorption of calcium and is needed for a healthy immune system. Because it is stored in the liver, a summer of moderate sun maybe enough to see some people through the winter as well. However, for most people in the UK, a supplement is required in the winter months. Fortified breakfast cereals, plant milk and vegetable margarines can be useful dietary sources if exposure to sunlight is not practicable.

FOODS AND DRINKS TO AVOID

If you are vegetarian or vegan then (wisely) you won't be eating fish; if you are not yet, then consider stopping! The government's Food Standards Agency (FSA) conservatively advises that pregnant and breastfeeding women should limit their consumption of oily fish to no more than two portions a week. They, along with children under 16, should avoid shark, marlin and swordfish entirely and limit the amount of tuna they eat due to contamination with potentially deadly pollutants.

There is overwhelming evidence highlighting the dangers of consuming deadly pollutants such as dioxins in herring, salmon, mackerel and, to a lesser degree, trout. Further, most of the world's fish are contaminated with mercury – a neurotoxin which causes neurological damage, developmental delays and learning difficulties.

The FSA also advises that pregnant women: "shouldn't take supplements containing cod liver oil, or other types of fish liver oil. This is because fish liver oil contains high levels of vitamin A, like liver and liver products such as liver pâtè. If you have too much vitamin A, levels could build up in your body and may harm an unborn baby."

Approximately 95 per cent of food poisoning cases are due to meat and dairy products. Remember, your baby will eat what you eat, so think carefully! Ripened soft cheeses such as Brie and Camembert must be avoided (and obviously will be if you're vegan!), as they may contain high levels of a bacteria called *listeria* which, in rare cases, can lead to listeriosis. This may result in miscarriage, still-birth or severe illness in the newborn baby. *Listeria* bacteria has also been found in a very small number of some cook-chill products. These must be reheated thoroughly until piping hot.

Eggs should be avoided as they carry risk of *Salmonella* and contain significant amounts of saturated fats and cholesterol.

Vegetables and salads should be washed thoroughly to remove any contaminated soil and dirt.

Buying organic fruit and veg will help to limit the chemicals, such as pesticides and herbicides, reaching your unborn baby.

Caffeine in coffee and fizzy drinks has been suspected of leading to birth defects or miscarriages but studies have proved inconclusive.

Although artificial sweeteners in food and drink are said to pose no threat, again there have been concerns regarding these. They cross the placenta and are eliminated very slowly from foetal tissues.

Smoking is clearly bad for you and your baby and is associated with low birth weight and cot death. It's never too late to give up.

Any prescribed or over-the-counter medication may prove harmful to the baby, even aspirin, paracetamol and cold remedies. If you don't really need them, the advice is don't take them. If you do, consult your doctor.

Avoid eating peanuts and nuts while pregnant or breastfeeding if you, your partner or a child in the immediate family come from an atopic family – see Notes on Nuts on page 9.

MOTHER NATURE KNOWS BEST

Don't forget that despite all the rules and advice, vegan women have been producing healthy, beautiful babies for thousands of years. Trust your body and Mother Nature to nurture your unborn baby. We are a great ape and essentially evolved to thrive on a vegan diet (see other Viva! guides, *Wheat-Eaters or Meat-Eaters?* and *Your Health in Your Hands* at viva.org.uk/resources. Veganism is the most natural diet in the world so have a little faith!

"From the moment I found out I was pregnant, I had no doubt I'd raise my child vegan. Good nutrition is the key to a healthy life and I knew that by feeding my baby a balanced healthy vegan diet they would thrive.

During my pregnancy I encountered several challenging experiences with medical professionals who knew very little about the vegan lifestyle. Viva!'s Vegan New Parents' Guide proved to be a fountain of knowledge and armed me with all the information I needed to educate myself and others on how easy and accessible veganism can be for mother and baby.

Pregnancy brings about so many new challenges. However, I was so glad to have the guide to provide practical and reliable nutritional information for pregnancy and beyond."

Siobhan Dolan

"I've had two healthy, vegan pregnancies, raised one vegan kiddo, Eric, who is now 10 years old, and I'll soon be weaning my second, Soren, who is five months. We also feed my partner's kids vegan when they're here half the week. I like that being vegan makes us more creative in the kitchen; the kids often cook with us, and we try out lots of different recipes and cuisines. Whenever there is a new vegan cookbook we all look through and choose new meals to try. We get really excited when new foods are launched, and look forward to trying them as a family, resulting in lots of chat and opinions! We feel like it keeps us all healthier and full of energy and the children eat a great variety of foods. I love that Eric doesn't even see meat as food! And of course our consciences are clear knowing we've caused no harm."

Felicity Richards

BREAST iS BEST

Breastfeeding is certainly the most natural form of nutrition during the infant's first year of life. Breastmilk is truly miraculous – the perfect food for baby which not only contains every nutrient needed but antibodies that bolster the baby's immune system. It is impossible to replicate the exact formula of breastmilk. Neither can a bottle replicate the closeness and skin contact which a baby gets when feeding from their mother. Besides, breastfeeding is so much easier and more practical than bottlefeeding. There's no sterilising equipment, no buying of milk powder, no heating of milk during the wee small hours and no chance of forgetting the baby's milk if you go out for the day. Also, if you're patient, it's a natural means of losing any extra pounds you've put on during pregnancy. The World Health Organisation (WHO) now recommends that most women should exclusively breastfeed their babies for six months. They conclude that in general this is the healthiest start to life for a baby.

There are many benefits for the baby too. Asthma, eczema and other allergies can all be triggered by dairy produce in cow's milk formula or in the breastfeeding mother's diet. Digestive problems, ear infections, respiratory problems and intestinal bleeding have also been linked to the consumption of dairy products by infants.

Also, if you are concerned about calcium – remember that cow's milk has evolved for calves, not humans! It contains four times too much calcium for a human baby. Nature never meant for us to drink it as infants or at any other time in our life! Three-quarters of the world's population do not consume dairy products as they are lactose intolerant. There are many studies showing that nations consuming very little dairy (such as Thailand) have considerably lower incidences of osteoporosis than nations which consume high amounts (such as the USA). Further, a review of the evidence on the effect of cow's milk on bone health (published in the *Journal of the American Academy of Pediatrics* in 2005) concluded that children and adolescents do not require cow's milk but instead must exercise regularly and eat plenty of fresh fruit and vegetables and avoid smoking, fizzy drinks and caffeine for strong bones and teeth. For more information see our guide, *Why You Don't Need Dairy* from **vivashop.org.uk**.

All good reasons why babies should be breastfed wherever possible. Although breastfeeding is natural there is a knack to it and it is a good idea to prepare yourself before the birth by reading some of the very good books which are now available.

THE PRACTICALITIES OF BREASTFEEDING

Wash your breasts as usual when you bath or shower but don't use soap as this can wash away the natural secretions which protect against soreness when the baby starts to suck. Get used to handling your breasts so that you don't feel awkward or embarrassed about this when the time comes to start breastfeeding.

The baby's suckling reflex is at its strongest in the first few hours after birth, so when your baby is handed to you it is a good idea to put them straight to your breast. If, however, for some reason you feel you can't do this, don't worry. Just try again quietly and gently a little later – perseverance and good support usually leads to success.

It's important to have your baby in the right position with the head slightly tipped back so that the chin is close to your breast and the lips are close to your nipple – 'chest to chest, chin to breast.' Brush their lips with your nipple until they open their mouth really wide, almost as if they're going to yawn. This may take several minutes so be patient. When it does happen, bring the baby's head quickly towards your breast so that they takes not just your nipple but a good mouthful of breast too.

If they are latched on properly you will see the jaw bone move as they suck. If not, slide your little finger into the corner of their mouth to break the sucking action and try again. It is very important that your baby should have opened their mouth wide enough and be close enough for you to enable them to take a large mouthful of breast. This means that your nipple is protected from friction and will not get sore.

Watch that your breast is not covering your baby's nose, making breathing difficult. Gently hold back your breast with your fingers if necessary. After your baby has finished feeding, dry your breasts carefully. If you have problems with leaking, cover them with breast pads. Some people advise putting cream on or using a spray but this is not recommended as it interferes with the delicate balance of natural secretions. Wash your nipples once a day without soap and keep them dry.

Giving short feeds as often as your baby will co-operate in the early days will give you both practice. During these early feeds, your baby is getting not the milk but the colostrum which protects them from disease and helps them to excrete the meconium from the bowel. Meconium is a sticky, black waste product which builds up during the time the baby is in the womb. The actual milk comes in a few days after birth – this might be the second, third or fourth day. The milk normally comes in quicker for second and subsequent babies, but this depends on how much sucking the baby has been able to do. The more you have been able to feed the baby, the more your breasts will have been stimulated and the quicker the milk will come in, although until it does, the colostrum will supply all your baby's needs.

When the milk does come, you may find that you are really 'bursting' and the process is rather messy! Giving frequent brief feeds from the beginning will help to minimise this engorgement. Just keep on feeding your baby completely on demand and your supply will quickly adjust to your baby's needs. If you find you have so much milk that it gushes out too quickly, making your baby splutter, you can hold back the milk a little by holding your breast in your fingers just above the nipple and pushing your breast gently upwards.

In the early days you might find that milk leaks from your breasts between feeds: even hearing the cry of another baby can trigger the 'let down reflex' which can cause this to happen. A breast pad inside your bra helps, as does wearing darkish tops which do not show up any wet patches too obviously. These inconveniences pass rapidly as you and your baby get used to breastfeeding. Your breasts will return back to their normal size (even though they are producing large quantities of milk), they will not leak and the whole process should become smooth, easy and quite delightful – very different from those early days of adjustment.

After your baby has finished feeding, hold them up against your shoulder and gently rub or pat their back until they burp. Make sure that they are upright, otherwise the wind will not come up. Some babies do not swallow much air so won't need to burp. Don't worry if nothing happens! And don't worry if your baby brings up some milk after feeds. This is quite normal and just means that they've had more than enough. However, if there is projectile vomiting (where it shoots across the room), you should consult a doctor as this may indicate a fault in the baby's stomach muscles which can be cured by a small operation.

Have confidence in your ability to breastfeed and don't give in without a really good try. There are so many wonderful benefits for both of you and don't forget ... practice makes perfect!

THE IDEAL DIET FOR PERFECT BREASTFEEDING

During breastfeeding, your need for extra vitamins and minerals continues as in pregnancy but you will also need more niacin, magnesium, phosphorus, zinc and selenium. Yeast extract, wholemeal bread, wholegrains, some pulses, avocado, seeds, nuts, mushrooms, brown rice, bananas, tofu and beansprouts are all good foods to boost your intake of these vitamins and minerals.

Just include one or two additional snacks each day made from fresh fruit and vegetables, nuts, pulses, black treacle, dried fruits, fortified soya products and yeast extract for high-powered, nutrient-rich feeding. If you are vegan always ensure a good supply of vitamin B12 by taking a daily supplement.

Your diet as a vegan breastfeeding mum will provide all the nutrients your baby needs. And there is one less risk to worry about.

FORMULA FEEDS

Never give cow's milk (whether full fat, semi or skimmed) – it is meant for calves and therefore contains the wrong proportions of nutrients for the human baby. For example it is too high in calcium and protein and too low in iron and essential fatty acids. This is why companies make millions of pounds turning cow's milk into cow's milk formulas – they alter the nutritional composition in an attempt to mimic human breast milk. Also do not give soya milk (or other plant milks) to a baby – it's too low in fat and too high in protein. If you want to use a formula, give soya milk formula until your child is about two years old.

Don't be in too much of a hurry to give supplementary bottles, something many mothers do because they doubt their own ability to produce enough milk. Your body responds to the baby's demands so if you start to give bottles, the baby takes less milk from you which means you produce less and have to give more bottles. Breastfeeding is best for babies and we recommend persevering with breastfeeding if you can. However we understand that for various good reasons you may need to bottlefeed your baby and choosing the right feed will naturally be important.

THE SOYA STORY FOR BABIES

Currently there are no completely animal-free soya infant formulas on the market suitable for young babies – as the vitamin D that is added is obtained from lanolin (a waxy substance in sheep wool). Contact the manufacturers to ask them to use non-animal vitamin D as consumer pressure may persuade them to change. However, soya formula is still far preferable to cow's milk formula, from a health perspective and for at least minimising animal cruelty.

The NHS states that from the age of one, you can give your baby unsweetened, calcium-fortified, plant-based drinks (such as soya, oat and almond milk) as part of a healthy balanced diet.

There is also is Alpro soya junior 1+ milk alternative which can be used as a main drink for children aged one onwards and as part of a balanced diet from six months. It is higher in calories (needed by toddlers) than normal soya milk and enriched with calcium, iron and non-animal vitamin D and is suitable for vegans.

There has been some concern over soya-based infant formulas in the media. The main concern has been the fact that soya beans contain compounds called isoflavones, or phytoestrogens, which behave like oestrogen, the female hormone. Ironically, many of the beneficial health effects of soya are attributed to the action of phytoestrogens (eg lowering blood pressure, reducing bad cholesterol, reducing menopausal symptoms and risk of diabetes). These natural plant hormones are found in

many foods. Examples of non-soya foods that contain phytoestrogens include cereals, bread, raisins, rice, chickpeas, haricot beans, butter beans, bean sprouts, fruits and mixed vegetable dishes. In other words, they are almost impossible to avoid – and shouldn't be avoided!

They may act in a similar way to the hormone oestrogen but they are much weaker, between 100 and 100,000 times weaker. In fact, scientists suggest that phytoestrogens may actually have a normalising effect on the body's natural oestrogen levels (this means they may raise levels when they are too low; and lower them when they are too high).

Cow's milk (and milk formula), however, contains real oestrogen – the same hormone that women produce. Raised levels of oestrogen from cow's milk are linked to breast cancer and prostate cancer. For more information see Viva!'s report *One in Nine*, which can be viewed at **viva.org.uk/resources**.

If a health professional were truly worried about the affects of oestrogen on a baby then cow's milk formula would be banned! And yet, it is soya formula that comes under attack for the much weaker oestrogen-like component it contains which is protective for human health.

BUT DOES THE AMOUNT OF SOYA A BABY EATS MATTER?

Again, a baby drinking cow's milk formula consumes much more oestrogen (the real thing) than a baby consuming soya formula. Infants consuming soya formula are not exposed to levels higher than those seen in many Asian countries. A UK government report acknowledges that there is no evidence that people who regularly eat high quantities of soya, such as Chinese and Japanese individuals, have altered sexual development or impaired fertility! It should be remembered that China is the world's most populous nation, with over 1.4 billion citizens, that have been consuming soya for more than 3,000 years!

For fuller information, see Viva!'s easy to read and informative guide, *The Soya Story,* available from **viva.org.uk/resources**.

Cow's milk contains a cocktail of over 35 different hormones and growth factors. Furthermore, modern dairy cows (including organically farmed cows) are frequently impregnated while still producing milk. At least two-thirds of retail milk in the UK is taken from pregnant cows whilst the hormone level in the milk is markedly elevated. Hormones from cow's milk are linked to breast and prostate cancers. Viva! wholeheartedly believe soya milk formula to be the safe option for babies.

TOOTH TRUTH

Infant soya formula may contain glucose syrup. All infant formulas must comply with standards laid down by UK Regulations which specify minimum and maximum amounts of carbohydrate (the body's main form of energy). The carbohydrate used can't be lactose (the sugar in cow's milk) so an alternative carbohydrate is used – glucose syrup. Glucose syrup comes from corn starch.

Tooth decay can be the result of many factors, not only the presence of sugars in a food or drink. Research has shown that soya infant formulas are no more likely to cause tooth decay than cow's milk infant formulas. The most important factor appears to be how they are consumed. Any food or drink containing sugars shouldn't have

frequent or prolonged contact with the teeth and trainer cups should be used as soon as your baby is able to drink this way. Thus if normal weaning practices are adopted, soya infant formulas (or other formulas) should not cause harm to teeth.

Soya infant formulas have been used for decades – indeed a review on this subject in *Nutrition Review* states that for more than 80 years, "soya-based infant formulas have been fed to millions of infants worldwide and studied in controlled clinical research… Consequently, soya-based infant formulas continue to be a safe, nutritionally complete feeding option for most infants".

Of course, soya is not a natural food for babies but then again, nor is cow's milk which is loaded with oestrogens – and not the mild ones derived from plants but potent oestrogens from another mammal. And we have already seen the host of illnesses and conditions that may be linked to infants consuming dairy products.

Our opinion is that we would choose soya formula milk to feed our babies (and did!) and consider soya milk to be a healthy food for both children and adults and far superior to cow's milk.

MAKiNG THE FORMULA

Making up the formula depends on the brand so make sure you read the label properly. Generally, the method is as follows: wash your hands first and boil enough water for the number of bottles you intend to make. When boiling the water empty the kettle and put in fresh water – water that has been boiled before may have levels of minerals that are too high. Let the water cool and then put the correct amount in each bottle, using the measure on the side. Measure the formula using the scoop provided. Don't pack it down as too much powder can be harmful. Level it off with a knife. Add the powder to the bottle, screw on the cap and shake to dissolve. Store the bottle in the fridge but throw any away that is not used after 24 hours.

Some babies like their formula straight from the fridge, others prefer a bottle warmed in a bottle warmer, microwave oven or jug of hot water. To give a bottle, cradle the baby in the crook of your arm so that they are cosy and close to you. When practical, open your shirt so that they can feel the warmth of your skin. Gently touch the baby's cheek nearest to you and as they turn towards you pop the teat in their mouth. Make sure you tilt the bottle well so that the milk fills the teat-end of the bottle and no air can get in which would give them colic. Pull on the bottle a little as your baby sucks, to keep up the suction. After your baby has finished their feed, 'burp' them as described at the end of the breastfeeding section.

Four To Six Months Old

At this age you can give your baby a little cooled, boiled water from a normal cup as a way of introducing them to water as a drink. Continue with breast or bottle feeding in the normal way.

Breast milk supplies all your baby's needs, including vitamin C, for the first six months of their life. So if your baby is happy and thriving, there is no need to think about introducing solids until they're six months old. However, if after four months your baby doesn't seem fully satisfied with milk, you might try giving a first taste of food – but don't start before four months old as introducing solids too early to an immature digestive system could cause an allergic reaction.

The NHS advise that there are three clear signs which, when they appear together from around six months of age, show that your baby is ready for their first solid foods, alongside breast milk or first infant formula.

They will be able to:

- stay in a sitting position, holding their head steady
- coordinate their eyes, hands and mouth so they can look at their food, pick it up and put it in their mouth
- swallow food (rather than spit it back out)

The first spoonfuls are really just to get your baby used to the taste and feel of solid food. Do not think of it as a real source of nourishment at this stage. The baby still needs milk feeds for that and the emotional satisfaction of suckling.

The first taste should be half a teaspoonful of a fruit or vegetable purée (see *Foods For Weaning and How to Prepare Them,* on page 48). Traditionally, cereals were always the first solid food given to babies, but these are now advised against due to the possibility of an allergic reaction when given so early. Allergic reactions are really quite rare and where they do occur, are usually inherited so you will know in advance if they are likely. Delaying the first solid food to four or six months lowers the risk of an allergic reaction because the digestive system is better able to cope.

The most common foods to cause allergies are cow's milk and dairy products, eggs, nuts, some fruits and foods containing gluten. Signs of an allergic reaction are rashes and swelling of the eyes, lips and face; sickness; diarrhoea; eczema; hay fever and asthma. Babies often grow out of allergies, usually by the time they are two years old, although some, particularly to dairy products and nuts, can last a lifetime.

Give this first taste of solids at one of the main milk feeds corresponding to breakfast, lunch or dinner, whichever is the most convenient. If you are planning to go back to work but want to continue breastfeeding, start giving the solids at lunchtime as this will eventually become the first meal at which the baby gives up breastfeeding and has only solids.

Whether you give the solid food before or after the milk feed is entirely up to you, or perhaps more to the point, up to the baby! It's generally better to give solids before the milk feed so you can gradually increase the quantity until the baby is satisfied and eventually forgets about the milk feed. However, there is no point in trying to give solid foods if your baby is hungry and crying, wanting comfort and crying for a feed. Better to feed first and give solids afterwards.

Use a flat, shallow spoon and be prepared for the fact that your baby may well spit out your lovingly prepared offerings. Don't take it personally and don't worry because the baby is not depending on it for nourishment at this stage. Try again another day, persisting gently. There is no hurry.

It's a good idea to try your baby on the same food for several days before introducing another so you can make sure there is no allergic reaction. Certainly if you have any history of allergies, asthma, eczema or hay fever in the family, it is advisable to continue with just one food for at least four days before trying another, and watching carefully for any reaction. You can gradually increase the quantity so that your baby is having, perhaps, two tablespoonfuls at a time. This allows the baby's digestive system to slowly adapt.

"As a lifelong veggie-turned-vegan, bringing our children up following a vegan lifestyle was second nature and, luckily, very supported by our families. My mother Cath turned vegan in 2017 after 40 years of vegetarianism, and my sister, aunt and nephew have all followed after seeing the benefits it has brought to the health and wellbeing of our family.

Initially, when Lily was born, my husband didn't follow a vegan or vegetarian lifestyle, but we both agreed to bring up our children as vegan since 'you can't un-eat meat' and they could follow their own paths when they are older (hopefully a continuation of the path they are on!). Tim embraced the vegan lifestyle over time and now no longer eats meat. After many years of managing health food stores I opened my own vegan shop, Brontosaurus Vegan, in 2017 with the hope of making veganism more accessible in my city.

Both of our children are proud vegans, they understand that we love animals so will never eat them and that it is important that we look after the planet now more than ever. They are compassionate, gentle and determined to change the world into a kinder place. As a family we eat a huge variety of food – we are currently exploring foods from different continents and learning how to recreate traditional dishes, but vegan. It has been an exciting and tasty way to hibernate during the pandemic."

Charlie Berry

FOODS FOR WEANING AND HOW TO PREPARE THEM

Carrot purée
Peel a carrot and boil it in a little unsalted water until tender; purée with enough of the cooking water to make a soft consistency. Start by giving a taste of half a teaspoonful before or after the midday or evening milk.

Swede or parsnip purée
Make like carrot purée.

Apple or pear sauce
Use sweet apples or pears only, not tart ones that require added sweetening. Peel, core and slice the fruit and cook in 2-3 tablespoons of water until tender. Purée, adding a little extra boiled water if necessary to make a soft consistency.

Banana
Mash the flesh of a very ripe banana thoroughly with a fork, adding a little cooled, boiled water if necessary to make a soft consistency.

Avocado
Cut in half, scoop out and mash the flesh, adding a few drops of cooled boiled water if necessary.

Courgette
Cut off the ends and cut into small pieces. Cook in a minimum of unsalted water until tender. Purée with enough cooking water to make a soft consistency.

Pumpkin
Peel and remove the seeds. Cut the flesh into pieces and cook in a little boiling water until tender. Purée.

Tomato
Suitable raw or cooked. Sieve cooked tomato to remove the seeds. Scald and peel raw tomato and cut out the core, then mash. You can remove the seeds if you like, but the jelly around them is a valuable source of soluble fibre.

Grated apple or pear
Choose sweet apples and well-ripened pears. Peel and grate finely.

Peaches, apricots, sweet cherries, mangoes, papaya, kiwi fruit
Choose really ripe fruit, remove the skin and pips or stones and mash the flesh thoroughly.

Broccoli, cauliflower, Brussels sprouts, green cabbage

Wash and trim. Cook in a minimum of unsalted water until tender (they should be mashable but not soggy). Purée with a little of their cooking water. (Cooked cabbage and brussels sprouts can create intestinal gas – if this is a problem, mix with another vegetable purée such as carrot.)

Spinach

Wash thoroughly, remove the stems and shred the leaves. Cook in a saucepan with a little extra water until spinach is tender. Purée. (Don't give more than once or twice a week as the oxalic acid content affects the body's absorption of some minerals.)

Dried apricots, prunes, pears, peaches, apples

Wash, then cover with boiling water and soak overnight. Next day, simmer until tender. Remove pits from prunes. Purée. (Can have a rather laxative effect.)

Date Purée

- 225g plain dates
- ½ cup water

Put the dates into a saucepan with the water and heat gently for 5 – 10 minutes, or until the dates are mushy. Remove from the heat and mash with a spoon to make a thick purée, looking out for and removing any stones as you do so; set aside to cool.

Baby rice cereal

This is the best first cereal to give because it is the least likely to cause allergic reactions. Choose one fortified with additional iron and B vitamins, and make up with liquid according to the directions on the pack.

Potatoes and sweet potatoes

Scrub. Bake or boil in unsalted water. Scoop potato out of the skins and mash. Very finely chopped green vegetables can also be added, such as watercress or raw spinach leaves. Or mashed tofu.

Corn, peas, green beans
Boil until tender and purée. Fresh or frozen are fine; canned are not advised because of the salt and sugar they contain.

Muesli
Buy a mix without sugar and other additives, or make your own from oats, nuts and raisins, then grind to a powder. Moisten with water, fruit juice or plain soya yoghurt. Sprinkle with wheatgerm, mix well. Powdered nuts, seeds or grated apple or pear can be added.

Wholemeal bread
From six months onward, a little crustless bread can be added to vegetable purées. The bran in 100 per cent wholemeal bread and flour is too laxative for some babies; a 50:50 bread (preferably with added wheatgerm for extra iron) or enriched white bread is often a better choice for babies under two years old.

BABY LED WEANING

In recent years, baby led weaning (BLW) has grown in popularity. It is a method of feeding that begins with offering your baby solid foods, instead of starting with purees, which are of a suitable texture and size for the age of your baby.

For a six-month-old baby, a starting point might be finger-shaped foods like a strip of melon or a small floret of cooked broccoli. Foods that are safe are ones that are soft enough to squish in between your finger and thumb, or that you can press against the roof of your mouth with your tongue. Babies don't need teeth to be able to chew solid foods.

Benefits of BLW are that your child can have more of the same foods as the rest of the family (with a few considerations), you spend less time making purées or less money on jarred baby foods. Babies weaned in this way often show a greater acceptance of different foods and textures.

Starting solid foods is a gradual process and some people combine some baby lead weaning with the introduction of some puréed or mashed foods, like banana or stewed apple for example. And some babies won't eat much at all at first and this is fine, because at this age they should still be getting all their nutritional needs met by their breast or bottle feeds.

A piece of banana with a small piece of peel left on can be a great place to start – the peel will help them get a grip a bit better for self-feeding. Slices of avocado can be another nice place to start.

NOTE:

Never leave a baby alone when they are eating finger foods or 'pieces' of food because of the danger of choking. If anything does get stuck in baby's throat, be ready to hook it out quickly with your finger or turn your baby upside down and smack gently in the small of the back.

Examples of foods for baby led weaning (in slices, fingers or florets)

- Avocado
- Very soft sweet potato
- Cooked butternut squash
- Cooked broccoli or cauliflower
- Toast sticks with hummus or smooth peanut butter
- Melon
- Banana

SUGGESTED FEEDING PATTERNS FROM FOUR TO SIX MONTHS OLD

On waking: Breast or bottle-feed.
Breakfast: Breast or bottle-feed.
Mid-morning: Cooled boiled water from a spoon or cup.
Lunch: ½ – 2 teaspoons of fruit or vegetable purée or if BLW, slice of avocado or melon for example. Breast or bottle feed.
Dinner: Breast or bottle-feed.
Before bed: Breast or bottle-feed.

Six to Eight Months Old

As your baby takes more solid food, the demand for milk will decrease. Your baby will suck from you for a shorter time and at around eight months may eventually give up the milk feed entirely at the meal time. Your milk supply will decline correspondingly, the reverse of the process that enabled you to produce enough milk in the early days. You will probably find it takes two or three days for your body to catch up with the baby's decrease in demand and your breasts may feel rather full, but this transition period only lasts for a couple of days or so.

You can now begin to enrich the simple fruit and vegetable purées with vegan protein ingredients. Any of the following can be added:

Red lentils made into a thick soup make a wonderfully nutritious meal for a baby. Serve it as it is or with a little crustless wholemeal bread mashed into it or make the soup extra thick and add to a vegetable purée.

Mashed beans such as soya, red kidney, cannellini or butter beans can be cooked thoroughly and mashed into a purée. Use home-cooked or canned ones but if using the latter, ensure they are rinsed properly to remove the salted water. Don't give canned beans to a baby younger than eight months.

Beans in tomato sauce make a nutritious meal from eight months onwards. Choose a variety without preservatives or colourings as although they will probably still contain a little sugar and salt, they remain a nutritious food. Mash or purée them. They can be mixed with crumbled wholemeal bread and a little boiled water to moisten.

Tahini or peanut butter can be mixed a little at a time into fruit or vegetable purées. Half a teaspoonful should be enough to start off with. Choose or make a smooth peanut butter without salt or additives. (Peanut butter should never be given directly on its own as it can cause choking.)

Yeast extract can be added one quarter of a teaspoon at a time, to vegetable purée. Use a low-sodium extract.

Brewer's yeast (a debittered one) can be sprinkled sparingly – say quarter of a teaspoonful – over baby's vegetable purée or breakfast muesli mix. It can also be added to mashed banana and yoghurt mix.

Finely milled nuts and seeds (milled in a food processor or clean electric coffee grinder or bought ready ground) can be stirred into fruit or vegetable purées, starting with half a teaspoonful. If you're grinding your own, use a variety of nuts: almonds, Brazil nuts, peanuts, walnuts, pumpkin and sunflower seeds.

Wheatgerm can be sprinkled over fruit or vegetable purées, added to cereal mixes and yoghurt for splendid nourishment.

Yoghurt – an active, plain soya yoghurt without preservatives – can be added to fruit purées or given with a sprinkling of wheatgerm or powdered nuts. It can be mashed with banana, wheatgerm, a little tahini and some powdered nuts to make a quick baby meal.

Once the baby is taking these solids happily, you can give an enriched vegetable purée as a main course, followed by a fruit purée, yoghurt or cereal-based mixture as a 'pudding'.

If you are doing BLW, you can try your baby on some small cubes of either raw or cooked firm tofu.

When they are taking different suitable finger foods happily, you could offer a piece of cooked vegetable and some small cubes of tofu for a main course for example and a piece of banana with some yoghurt as a 'pudding'.

You can also begin introducing solids before the other main feeds of the day, so that eventually the feeds that correspond to breakfast, lunch and dinner are composed entirely of solids. If you have been puréeing some foods, you may find as your baby gets used to different textures, you may be able to offer them whole.

You will gradually be able to drop first one milk feed and then another so that by the time your baby is around nine months, the bedtime feed may well be the only one left. Do not be in a hurry to wean your baby from the bliss of this; it is important for the closeness to you and the emotional satisfaction that suckling gives. Many babies have spontaneously given up on the bedtime feed by the time they are one year old, but many have not.

There are those who believe you shouldn't encourage feeding during the night after, say, six months, when your baby probably doesn't need it for nourishment. Your baby may just be acquiring an enjoyable habit that may eventually drive you to distraction. Other child-care experts disagree with this and our view is that if a child cries for food and the loving comfort of their mother's closeness, then

it is better to meet that need, even though it can be demanding. But it does pass and contributes very much to the child's emotional security, both at the time and in later life.

Some people believe that when you start to give solid food, that is the time to wean a baby from the breast to the bottle. We don't see any point in this unless you want to stop breast-feeding. If your baby is happy and all is going well, it seems better to continue breast-feeding for the few remaining months. However, once your baby has given up all the daytime feeds, you might like to give a bottle for the final feed so that others can also give this food.

Once your baby starts teething, they may find it comforting to chew on something hard: a piece of apple, raw carrot, bread or rusk. Again, supervision when eating these sorts of foods is recommended due to the danger of choking.

SUGGESTED FEEDING PATTERNS FROM SIX TO EIGHT MONTHS OLD

On waking: Breast or bottle-feed.
Breakfast: Baby rice or muesli cereal or enriched fruit purée; breast or bottle-feed.
Mid-morning: Cooled boiled water from a spoon or cup.
Lunch: 1-2 tablespoons enriched vegetable purée, or lentil purée, followed by some fruit purée (optional). Or if BLW, cooked carrot fingers with small cubes of firm tofu or toast fingers and low-salt hummus.
Finger Foods: Slices of apple or cucumber.
Dinner: Same as breakfast; breast or bottle-feed.
Before Bed: Breast or bottle-feed.

Eight to Twelve Months Old

If your baby takes well to solids, you will quite soon find that they will easily and naturally eat a little of what you, as a family, are having. The main thing to watch (apart from avoiding sugar, salt, caffeine, deep fried foods and additives for under twos) is that the baby's portion is not too highly seasoned. Sometimes it's possible to take out a small quantity for the baby before adding spices and seasonings.

If your baby gets used to trying new flavours, it will make it possible for you to eat out with friends or in a restaurant. Simply select a suitably unspiced or lightly seasoned dish from the menu and mash the baby's portion with a fork.

At this stage you may need to consider the amount of fibre your baby is getting. Since a vegan diet is naturally high in fibre, which facilitates the passage of food through the intestines, it's important for the baby to have some concentrated sources of nourishment each day as well, such as powdered nuts, yeast and yeast extract (unsalted), tahini, peanut butter and yoghurt. If the diet becomes too laxative, it can cause a very sore bottom and reduce the amount of nutrients being absorbed. It is advisable to give a bread that is lower in fibre than wholemeal. Try wheatgerm bread or, if this is still too fibrous, buy a 50:50 or an enriched white one. Try a higher fibre bread again when your baby is a little older.

SUGGESTED FEEDING PATTERNS FROM EIGHT OR NINE MONTHS ON

At this stage, between nine months and a year, your baby will probably have an eating plan that goes something like this:

On waking: Water from a cup.
Breakfast: Muesli or oatmeal; toast or bread with low-sodium yeast extract.
Mid-morning: Water from a cup
Lunch: Mashed nut or bean or lentil savoury with vegetables; fruit purée and cereal pudding or fruit with yoghurt. Water. If BLW, cooked pasta shapes with large pieces of sliced tomato or avocado, followed by a piece of banana and yoghurt.
Mid-afternoon: Water; finger foods – apple, carrot, pear.
Dinner: Bread with nut butter, yeast extract or lentil spread or lentil soup with bread; carrot sticks, pieces of raw cucumber, slices of apple; fruit with yoghurt or cereal pudding.
Before Bed: Breast or bottle-feed.

Survival Tips

Don't worry if your child really does not like some food; you can usually find another source of the same nutrients. It's better to stick to foods that you know will go down well and avoid a battle of wills.

All children will go through the stage when they learn the power of the word no! If this veto is used over food you may be able to nip it in the bud by offering a choice of two equally nutritious items instead of one that they can veto.

Encourage your toddler to feed themself from an early age. Yes, it's horribly messy but a sensible bib – the plastic ones with pockets which catch spilled foods – is good and some kind of easily washed covering on the floor under the baby's chair will cope with most disasters.

Don't worry if your toddler eats the foods in the 'wrong' order or mixes things up (after all, that's part of the fun, spoilsport!) and don't set too high a standard. Your toddler will enjoy being independent and competence will grow with practice.

If there's a problem over food, the secret is not to get emotional about it. It simply isn't worth making an issue over food or allowing difficult situations to develop. In fact, as in all things concerning your child, it's your relationship with them that's most important. This is what you're building up and what will endure long after you've forgotten the horrors of broken nights, food fads and puddles on the carpet! Always put your relationship first, before a spotless house, before rigid time-tables, before battles over food and you will be rewarded by the deepening bond of understanding and companionship that will develop between you.

From the age of one you can give your baby unsweetened, calcium-fortified, plant-based drinks (such as soya, oat and almond drinks) as part of a healthy balanced diet. Introduce plant-based milks one at a time, in very small amounts so you can spot any allergic reaction.

Viva!'s Recipes for Toddler (and You!)

by Helen Wilson

TOFU AND POTATO CAKES

Recommended age of child: From one year
Preparation time: 10 mins
Cooking time: 15 mins
Serves: 2-4

These soft little savoury cakes with potato, tofu and parsley are just super for little fingers to get stuck into… but nice for adults too, with a bit more seasoning!

- 250g/9 oz potatoes, peeled and cut into even sized chunks
- 15g/½ oz vegan margarine or 1 tbsp oil
- A little soya or other unsweetened plant milk
- 100g/4 oz firm tofu
- 1-2 tbsp chopped parsley
- Freshly ground black pepper, to taste
- A little flour
- Rapeseed/veg oil

1 Boil the potatoes until tender, then drain and mash with the margarine/oil and a little plant milk if necessary.
2 Mash the tofu and then add to the potato, along with the parsley and pepper to taste.
3 Form the mixture into four flat cakes, coat with flour, then either brush with oil and grill on both sides or shallow-fry.
4 Drain on kitchen paper and serve when they have cooled down a little. Chop into small pieces for younger children.

LENTIL SOUP

Recommended age of child: from six months
Preparation time: 5 mins
Cooking time: 30 mins. Speed it up using a pressure cooker.
Serves: 2-4

Very soothing and nourishing as well as an excellent source of iron. This soup is very popular with babies and toddlers.

- 225g/8 oz red lentils
- 1 onion, peeled and finely chopped
- 2 garlic cloves, peeled and chopped
- 2 tbsp vegan margarine
- Juice half a lemon
- Salt (optional – avoid if cooking for babies/young children)
- Black pepper
- 1 tsp ground cumin (optional)

1 Put the lentils, onion and garlic into a saucepan with 1 litre (1¾ pints) water.
2 Bring to the boil and then simmer for about 30 minutes, until the lentils are very tender and pale. Or cook them in a pressure cooker on high for 5 minutes.
3 Stir well to get a smooth texture. Then add some lemon juice (start with 1 tablespoon), season as required and serve.

NO SALT/LOW—SALT HUMMUS

Recommended age of child: From six months
Preparation time: 5 mins
Serves: 1 large portion to be used across several meals

You can buy hummus practically everywhere these days – but it's cheap and simple to make your own and you can leave out the salt, or just add a tiny pinch, when making it for kids.

- 1x 400g tin chickpeas, drained and rinsed
- 1-2 cloves garlic, peeled and roughly chopped
- 2 tbsp tahini
- 2 tbsp lemon juice
- 2 tbsp olive oil
- 4 tbsp water
- Pinch of salt (optional)

1 Blend all the ingredients together in a blender or using a stick blender in a jug. Add a bit more oil or water for a thinner consistency.

KiDS' PASTA

Recommended age of child: From 18 months
Preparation time: 5 mins
Cooking time: According to packet instructions
Serves: 4

This is a very easy and popular kids' pasta recipe with lots of different protein options! It's great in lunchboxes too.

- 250g/9 oz kid-friendly pasta shapes
- 200g/2 cups mixed frozen veg
- ½ red pepper, diced (optional)
- Handful vegan cheese, grated (optional)
- 100g/3½ oz spinach (optional)
- Optional protein extras: fried vegan chicken strips/pieces (cooked according to packet), mixed seeds (sunflower, pumpkin, sesame), marinated tofu pieces (eg Cauldron), chopped up 'sausage', pine nuts, edamame beans, nutritional yeast

Dressing
- Either: use a shop-bought vegan pesto (eg Sacla or Zest) or mix 2 tbsp olive oil with 1 tsp syrup (eg maple or agave) and ¼ tsp mustard

1 Cook the pasta according to the instructions on the packet and then add the frozen vegetables and spinach into the water 3-5 minutes before the pasta is ready.
2 Drain the pasta.
3 Stir through the red pepper, protein option and dressing, then sprinkle with vegan cheese.

IOLO'S AVOCADO PASTA

Recommended age of child: From 10 months
Preparation time: 5 mins
Cooking time: according to pasta packet instructions
Serves: 2

Helen's son Iolo is nine years old and this is the first dinner he learned to cook by himself (with a little help and supervision). It makes a tasty and nutritious dinner in very little time. Popular with younger children too!

- 100g/3½ oz of child-friendly pasta shapes
- 1 large ripe avocado
- 1 lime, juiced
- 1 tbsp olive oil
- 6 cherry tomatoes, halved
- ¼ cucumber, sliced into disks

1 Cook the pasta in a saucepan, according to the packet instructions.
2 Meanwhile, half and carefully stone the avocado and scoop it out into a bowl and mash roughly with a fork.
3 Mix the lime juice and olive oil in with the avocado.
4 Drain the pasta and then tip it back into the saucepan. Spoon the mashed avocado into the pasta and then mix everything together thoroughly.
5 Divide into two small bowls and decorate with the tomatoes and cucumber.

SiMPLE 'YELLOW RiCE' KiTCHEREE

Recommended age of child: From eight months
Preparation time: 5 mins
Cooking time: 30 mins
Serves: 2-4

This cheeky little recipe is a great way of getting some protein-packed lentils into little stomachs! The lentils combine with the rice and turmeric to give a lovely colour.

- 75g/ ½ cup basmati rice, rinsed well
- 75g/ ½ cup red lentils, rinsed well
- 400ml/ 1¾ cups of water
- ¼ tsp ground turmeric
- 1 tsp cumin seeds
- 1 tsp low-salt vegetable stock eg Kallo
- 1 clove garlic, roughly chopped
- 2cm fresh ginger, roughly chopped (optional)
- Handful fresh spinach (optional)
- 2 tsp vegan margarine (eg Pure, Vitalite or Naturli)

1 Put the rice and lentils into a medium/large saucepan with 250ml of the water and bring it to the boil.
2 Turn down to simmer on a low/medium heat and stir in the rest of the ingredients, apart from the remaining water, spinach and margarine.
3 Stir occasionally to prevent it sticking to the base of the pan and as the liquid is absorbed by the kitcheree, add in more water a little at a time, as you would with a risotto.
4 Cook in this manner for around 30 minutes until you have a smooth consistency and the rice and lentils are thoroughly cooked and mixed together. Add more water to make it thinner if you desire.
5 Stir in the fresh spinach if using and serve into bowls, topping with a teaspoon of vegan margarine on each.
NB: It's also great spread onto toast, like pâté, when it's gone cold!

CHOCOLATE AND BANANA NICE CREAM

Recommended age of child: From one year
Preparation time: 5 mins
Serves: 2-4

Healthy, delicious and made in under five minutes! The perfect quick treat.

- 4 ripe bananas, cut into chunks, frozen for 2 hours
- 3-4 tbsp plant milk
- 1 tbsp cocoa powder
- Chopped nuts, sauce or berries (optional)

1 Place all the ingredients together in a food processor or blender and blend until smooth. Add more milk to make it smoother if you need.
2 Serve with any of the optional toppings. You could also flavour by combining with mixed frozen berries or peanut butter, for example.

SCRAMBLED TOFU

Recommended age of child: From one year
Preparation/cooking time: 10 mins
Serves: 1-2

- 1 tsp vegetable oil
- 1 clove garlic, peeled and crushed OR ½ – 1 tsp garlic purée
- 175g/6 oz firm silken tofu
- 1 tsp tahini
- 1 tbsp tamari (gluten-free) or shoyu
- 1 tbsp nutritional yeast flakes
- ½ tsp ground turmeric
- Sliced avocado, sliced tomato, lightly cooked cherry tomatoes, alfalfa sprouts, chopped peppers or chilli, rocket or kale (optional)

1 Gently fry the garlic in the oil for about 30 seconds until lightly golden. Don't let it burn.
2 Add the all other ingredients and mix together. Try not to break the tofu up too much but make sure it's well stirred.
3 Heat to warm through for approximately 3-5 minutes and serve immediately.

TOFU 'EGG' MAYO WRAPS

Recommended age of child: From one year
Preparation time: 10 mins
Serves: 4

These magical wraps look and taste pretty much like the traditional egg mayonnaise equivalent – and the filling takes but a moment to make! There are several brands of vegan mayo out in the shops now, or make your own.

- 225-250g/8 oz firm tofu, crumbled or mashed with a fork
- 1 red onion, finely chopped (use pre-chopped if short of time)
- 1 tsp wholegrain mustard
- 1 tsp ground turmeric
- 3 tbsp vegan mayo (eg Hellman's, Heinz, Follow Your Heart, supermarket own-brands)
- 2 tsp nutritional yeast flakes (Engevita)
- Salt and pepper, to taste – if you want more of an eggy taste, use Kala Namak black salt
- Cress, or else use scissor-chopped chives or rocket

1 Mix all ingredients together in a bowl and then season to taste.
2 Spread a wrap with vegan margarine then a couple of tablespoons of tofu egg mayo and top with the chives, rocket or cress. Tuck in the sides and then roll up into a cylinder shape. Chop into three small pieces and serve with some chopped tomatoes or cucumber on the side.

MiNi SMOOTHiE BOWLS

Recommended age of child: From six months
Preparation time: 5 mins
Serves: 2

- 1 banana, chopped into pieces
- 125g/1 cup frozen or fresh berries (defrost slightly first if using frozen)
- 350ml/1½ cups plant milk of your choice
- 1 tsp peanut butter
- 80g/1 cup of oats
- 2 tbsp vegan yoghurt (eg Alpro or supermarket own brand – optional)

1 Using either a blender or a stick blender in a tall jug, blend together the banana, berries, milk and peanut butter until smooth. Add more milk if you prefer a runnier texture.
2 Split the oats equally between two cereal bowls and then spoon in smoothie into each, next to the oats.
3 Top with a spoonful of yoghurt, a couple of whole berries, some extra sliced banana or mixed seeds (optional).

MINI JACKET POTATOES WITH VEGAN CHEESE AND BEANS

Recommended age of child: From 10 months
Preparation time: 5 mins
Cooking time: 1 hour
Serves: 2

These tasty little jacket potatoes become even more appetising for little ones if you scoop out the cooked potato and mix it with some grated vegan cheese! A great supper to get going in advance at the end of the afternoon.

- 2 small jacket potatoes
- 2 tsp vegan margarine
- 4 tbsp grated vegan cheese
- 1 tin low-salt baked beans

1 Preheat oven to 180°C/350°F/Gas Mark 4.
2 Put the potatoes on a small baking tray in the oven and bake for around one hour, until they are soft throughout when you test with a knife.
3 Remove them from the oven and set aside while you heat through the baked beans.
4 Partially slit the potatoes open and using a tablespoon, scoop a good amount of potato from each into a bowl.
5 Mix in the margarine and vegan cheese until everything starts to melt together.
6 Spoon the potato mixture back into the jackets and serve each one onto a plate. Either top with baked beans or serve them on the side in a little bowl.

BROCCOLI AND POTATO SOUP

Recommended age of child: from one year
Preparation time: 5 mins
Cooking time: 30 mins
Serves: 2-4

Soups are a great way to introduce your child to different vegetables. Make a batch and freeze in small containers, to be defrosted when needed.

- 2 tbsp olive oil
- 1 onion, peeled and finely chopped
- 1 clove garlic, crushed
- 1 head broccoli, separated into florets (fresh or frozen)
- 200g/7 oz potatoes, peeled and cubed
- 1 leek, thinly sliced
- 500ml/2 cups vegetable stock (using a stock cube or vegetable bouillion)

1 Heat oil in a large saucepan and add the onion, fry on a medium heat until soft, adding the garlic after a few minutes.
2 Add the broccoli, potatoes and leek and keep stirring for a couple of minutes.
3 Add stock, bring to boil, then cover and turn down to simmer for 30 minutes.
4 Blend before serving to small children as it is easier to feed them or for them to spoon into their mouths.
5 Serve with 50 per cent wholemeal bread buttered with peanut or other nut butter.

FABULOUS FALAFEL

Recommended age of child: From 2 years
Preparation time: 5 mins
Cooking time: 45 mins
Serves: 4

Falafel is a traditional Middle Eastern or Mediterranean snack, often sold as street food and increasingly found in the UK – either at takeaways or sold in shops. However, the home-made version is hard to beat – cheap too! It's particularly easy if you have a deep-fat fryer but an old saucepan or wok plus basket or slotted spoon will do the trick. Don't omit the chilling stage – it will help the mixture to firm up enough to fry.

- 2 tbsp flaxmeal (ground flax seeds/linseeds) mixed with 3-4 tbsp warm water to make 2 flax 'eggs'. Set aside while you get the rest of the ingredients together

- 400g tinned chickpeas, rinsed and drained (don't throw away the chickpea water – it can be used for baking and vegan meringues!)
- 1 onion, finely chopped
- 2 tbsp parsley, finely chopped

- Juice of 1 lemon
- 4 garlic cloves, crushed
- 1 tsp ground coriander
- 1 tsp ground cumin
- ½ tsp salt
- Freshly ground black pepper
- ½ tsp ground turmeric
- ¼ tsp chilli or cayenne powder
- 1 tsp baking powder

- 100g/generous 3oz plain flour – half and half wholemeal to white flour is the best. Gluten free option: replace with GF flour but include 2 tbsp sieved gram flour in it
- Vegetable oil for frying – use a wok or shallow saucepan and pour enough oil to make it about 8-10 cm deep. Easier still, use a deep-fat fryer!

1 Combine the chickpeas, onion, parsley, lemon juice, garlic, coriander, cumin, salt, pepper, turmeric and chilli powder. Blend the mixture until it forms a smooth paste, scraping the sides of the bowl as needed – you want it to have some texture, not too smooth so use the pulse button rather than continuous. That way you can control the texture. Stop the machine to scrape down the sides occasionally so everything gets mixed in. (You can use a stick blender if you don't have a processor, but it's a little more hard work).

2 Transfer mixture to a large bowl and mix in the baking powder, flour and flaxmeal mixture. Season to taste with salt and freshly ground pepper. Spoon a dollop of dough and pinch it onto a baking sheet or tray lined with baking parchment – it's too sloppy to form into balls at this point. Chill in the fridge for 20 minutes+ until firm. If you intend to serve them immediately, preheat the oven to 180°C/350°F/Gas Mark 4. This will keep each batch of falafels warm while you cook the subsequent batches.

3 If you've got a deep-fat fryer, go for it. If not, heat the oil for frying in the wok or shallow saucepan. It should spit if you drop a teeny piece of batter in it.

4 Fry the falafels in separate batches until golden brown on all sides, about 3 minutes. Don't try to cram too many in the pan as this will cool down the oil and make them soggy. Remove with a slotted spoon and drain on kitchen paper before serving. Serve with pitta bread slices, hummus and slices of red pepper.

STiR—FRiED VEG AND TOFU WiTH RiCE

Recommended age of child: From one year
Preparation time: 5 mins
Cooking time: 15 mins
Serves: 2

A great way to introduce children to some new veg. Chop the veg thinly and stir fry in a little sesame oil or vegetable oil and serve with rice, or noodles.

- 210g/1 cup of rice
- 6 x 2cm cubes of firm tofu
- 4 green beans
- ¼ red and/or yellow pepper, thinly sliced
- ¼ small carrot, cut into thin slices
- 1 tsp sesame or vegetable oil

1 Rinse the rice and then cook according to the packet instructions.
2 Chop the tofu and slice the vegetables as directed above.
3 Meanwhile, heat the oil in a small frying pan and stir fry the vegetable pieces until soft.
4 Set aside and serve with the rice when it is cooked.

Other vegetables to try include; mini corn, mange tout, slices of mushroom and courgette. You could add a bit of low-salt soya sauce into the mix too.

90

Mini Fluffy Pancakes

Recommended age of child: From eight months
Makes: 12 small pancakes
Preparation time: 5 mins
Cooking time: 10 mins

This recipe is inspired by a Canadian pancake recipe Helen was given years ago by Demuths Cookery School in Bath. We've used it ever since, but here it's been adapted to make tiny pancakes for children.

- 100g/ 1 cup + 2 tbsp plain white flour
- ¼ tsp salt
- ½ tsp baking powder
- ¼ tsp bicarbonate of soda
- 5 tbsp plain, unsweetened vegan yoghurt
- 1 tbsp maple syrup
- 100ml soya milk
- 1 tbsp sunflower oil
- Optional topping: berries, yoghurt, slices of banana, maple syrup

1 Mix together the plain flour with the salt, baking powder and bicarbonate of soda.

2 Mix together the plain yoghurt, maple syrup and soya milk and pour this into the flour, whisking well until you have a smooth thick batter.

3 To cook the pancakes, heat a drop of sunflower oil in a large frying pan, swirl the oil around to cover the whole frying pan.

4 Drop several, one tablespoon sized dollops of pancake batter around the frying pan. Over a medium heat cook until the underside of the pancake is golden and bubbles have appeared throughout (about 30 seconds). You might be able to cook around eight mini pancakes at a time.

5 Loosen the pancakes by shaking the pan and then flip each pancake over and cook for a further 20 seconds.

6 Continue until you have finished the mix.

7 Serve several mini pancakes on top of each other on plates and ask the kids what they'd like to top them with!

QUICK AND HEALTHY MAC AND CHEESE

Recommended age of child: From one year
Preparation time: 10 mins
Cooking time: 15 mins
Serves: 2-4

This sauce is unbelievably cheesy and creamy and kids' would never guess that it contains carrots!

Pasta
- 300g/3 cups macaroni plus water for cooking (use gluten-free if necessary)

Cheese Sauce
- 225g /1¼ cup carrots
- 650-700g/4 cups potatoes
- 170ml/⅔ cup olive oil
- 170ml/⅔ cup water
- 40g/1 cup nutritional yeast
- 2 tbsp lemon juice
- 3 tsp salt
- Chopped tomato, spinach or toasted breadcrumbs (optional)

Pasta
1 Bring the macaroni to the boil and then simmer according to the instructions on the packet or to your preferred texture.

Cheese Sauce
1 Peel the potatoes and carrots and cut them into small chunks. In a large saucepan, bring them to the boil and then simmer until soft (around 15 minutes).
2 Drain the water and then add them to the blender.
3 Add all the other ingredients to the blender and then blitz until really smooth.
4 Add the cheese sauce straight onto the pasta and stir through until fully covered.
5 Add any of the optional extras or enjoy the dish on it's own... it's great either way!

POLENTA PIZZA BITES

Recommended age of child: From 10 months
Preparation time: 10 mins
Cooking time: 10-12 mins
Serves: 2

These little pizza bites are easy to make and the kids can help!
The toppings listed are just suggestions – you could add some
vegan meat-style slices chopped into pieces, pineapple or sweetcorn,
for example.

- ½ packet (250g) of ready-made polenta eg Ital Fresco
- 1 small jar of pizza topping sauce
- 1 packet of grated vegan cheese (eg Violife, Sheeze or supermarket own brands)
- 2 mushrooms, finely chopped
- 1-2 baby corns, finely sliced
- 1cm strip of red or yellow pepper, finely chopped
- 4 olives, finely chopped (optional)

1 Preheat oven to 180°C/350°F/Gas Mark 4.
2 Line a small baking tray with parchment.
3 Cut the polenta into small rectangles.
4 Place them on the baking tray and into the oven for 2 minutes.
5 Remove from the oven and turn them over with a spatula.
6 Spread each one with ½ teaspoon of pizza sauce and then decorate with toppings of your choice and a pinch of vegan cheese on each.
7 Bake the pizza bites in the oven for 10-12 minutes.
8 Serve with a bit of salad and/or a dollop of vegan mayonnaise or hummus.

RAW VEG PLATTER WITH HUMMUS AND TOAST FINGERS

Recommended age of child: From eight months
Serves: 2
Preparation time: 5 mins

Healthy meals for kids don't have to be time consuming and complicated. This platter is a quick and easy lunch or light supper option, which is nutritious and also gets kids into eating raw veg! Swap out any veg that you know your little ones definitely won't eat, but do try and re-introduce things sometimes! Halve the recipe for one child.

- 1 carrot, peeled and cut lengthways into four long pieces
- ¼ cucumber, cut lengthways into four long pieces
- 4 small florets of raw broccoli and/or cauliflower
- 4 cherry tomatoes, halved
- 2 pieces wholemeal bread
- 4 tbsp hummus, either homemade or low-salt if possible for babies and toddler
- Optional: Handful of cubed, raw, firm tofu and/or chunks of vegan cheese

1 Chop up all your veg and arrange equally between two plates.
2 Toast the bread and cut into 'soldiers' for dipping into the hummus and arrange around the vegetables.
3 Spoon 2 tablespoons of hummus onto each plate and serve.

Options: lots of kids love raw, firm tofu and it's a great protein source. Add some cubes of tofu to the platter, and/or chunks of vegan cheese.

RiCE CAKES WiTH MANY DiFFERENT TOPPiNG iDEAS!

Recommended age of child: From one year

Be sure to select low-salt rice cakes or varieties for children – not the highly flavoured ones.

Base ideas
- Vegan cream cheese
- Vegan chocolate spread
- Vegan meat-style slices
- Peanut butter
- Hummus

Toppings
- Avocado
- Cucumber
- Tomato
- Grated carrot
- Banana
- Blueberries
- Raisins

Two weeks' menu for your toddler's lunch and dinner

(Dishes marked * are suitable for freezing. Only give nuts if not from an atopic family – see page 9, *Note on Nuts*)

WEEK ONE

Recommended age of baby given at the start of each recipe

MONDAY

Lunch
- Tofu Potato Cakes and carrot sticks.
- Segments of orange.
- Breast milk or soya milk formula.

Dinner
- Bread with almond butter or tahini dip and slices of tomato.
- Grated apple with soya yoghurt and raisins.
- Breast milk or soya milk formula.

TUESDAY

Lunch
- Lentil Soup* with 50 per cent wholemeal bread mashed into it. Slices of tomato. Fresh fruit prepared for finger feeding.
- Breast milk or soya milk formula.

Dinner
- Low-salt Hummus* with broccoli florets, carrot sticks and wholemeal toast.
- Slices of apple.
- Breast milk or soya milk formula.

WEDNESDAY

Lunch
- Kids' Pasta* with nutritional yeast flakes or ground almonds.
- Finely grated apple with a little soya yoghurt.
- Breast milk or soya milk formula.

Dinner
- Reheated Lentil Soup* and wholemeal roll.
- Raw broccoli florets.
- Ripe pear slices.
- Breast milk or soya milk formula.

THURSDAY

Lunch
- Low-salt hummus* with fingers of 50 per cent wholemeal toast.
- Carrot sticks.
- Banana mashed with a little soya yoghurt.
- Breast milk or soya milk formula.

Dinner
- Mashed potato with some pieces of vegan sausage and peas (from one year).
- Carrot sticks.
- Mango slices.
- Breast milk or soya milk formula.

FRIDAY

Lunch
- Iolo's Avocado Pasta.
- Muesli: soya yoghurt mixed with rolled oats, finely grated apple and raisins.
- Breast milk or soya milk formula.

Dinner
- Simple 'Yellow Rice' Kitcheree.
- Chocolate and Banana Nice Cream.
- Breast milk or soya milk formula.

SATURDAY

Lunch
- Scrambled Tofu on crumbled 50 per cent wholemeal bread.
- Segments of orange.
- Breast milk or soya milk formula.

Dinner
- Red Kidney Bean and Avocado Salad with shredded lettuce and carrots sticks.
- Fingers of 50 per cent wholemeal bread with yeast extract.
- Slices of apple.
- Breast milk or soya milk formula.

SUNDAY

Lunch
- Tofu 'Egg' Mayo Wraps.
- Leftover smoothie (if you make the Mini Smoothie Bowl earlier).
- Breast milk or soya milk formula.

Dinner
- Mini Jacket Potatoes with Vegan Cheese and Beans.
- Apples with Raisins.
- Breast milk or soya milk formula.

WEEK TWO

MONDAY

Lunch
- Broccoli and Potato Soup*
  with Nut Butter on fingers of
  50 per cent wholemeal bread.
- Slices of apple.
- Breast milk or soya milk formula.

Dinner
- Fabulous Falafel*.
- Berries pureed with yoghurt
  or banana.
- Raw broccoli florets.
- Breast milk or soya milk formula.

TUESDAY

Lunch
- Left over Falafel*.
- Puréed apple with raisins.
- Soya milk formula.

Dinner
- Stir-Fried Vegetables, Rice and
  Tofu.
- Fresh fruit prepared for finger
  feeding.
- Breast milk or soya milk formula.

WEDNESDAY

Lunch
- Mini Fluffy Pancakes.
- Slices of melon.
- Breast milk or soya milk formula.

Dinner
- Quick and Healthy Mac and
  Cheese.
- Slices of banana and apple.
- Breast milk or soya milk formula.

THURSDAY

Lunch
- Left over Healthy Mac and
  Cheese.
- Chocolate and Banana Nice
  Cream.
- Breast milk or soya milk formula.

Dinner
- Polenta Pizza Bites.
- Sliced grapes (always cut
  grapes to avoid choking).
- Breast milk or soya milk formula.